Sometimes People March

by
TESSA
ALLEN

Balzer + Bray
An Imprint of HarperCollins *Publishers*

Balzer + Bray is an imprint of HarperCollins Publishers.

Sometimes People March
Copyright © 2020 by Tessa Allen
All rights reserved. Manufactured in Italy.
No part of this book may be used or reproduced in any manner whatsoever
without written permission except in the case of brief quotations embodied
in critical articles and reviews. For information address HarperCollins
Children's Books, a division of HarperCollins Publishers, 195 Broadway,
New York, NY 10007.
www.harpercollinschildrens.com

Libary of Congress Control Number: 2019953359
ISBN 978-0-06-299118-8

The artist used ink and watercolor to create the illustrations for this book.
Typography by Dana Fritts
Title lettering by Aurora Parlagreco
20 21 22 23 24 RTLO 10 9 8 7 6 5 4 3 2 1
❖
First Edition

For my family,
who have always encouraged me
to be feisty and curious

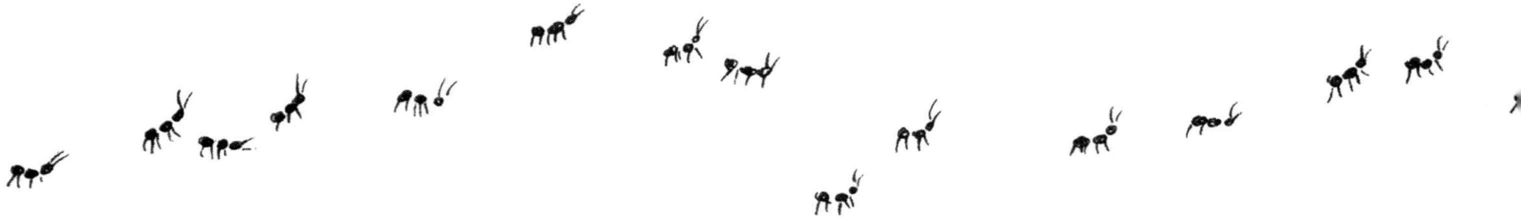

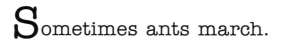

Sometimes ants march.

Sometimes bands march.

Sometimes people march.

Marching is something people do together
when they want to resist injustice

or when they notice the need for change.

People march for many reasons.

People march for things they care about

and people they love.

People march for the health of their bodies
and their communities and the world.

People march for
the freedom to love

and live

and learn.

Sometimes people carry signs to share their stories of resistance.

People resist in many ways.

Sometimes people resist
with their voices.

They might resist with words

or with songs

or art.

People resist with meetings.

They resist by
standing up

or sitting down

or taking a knee.

It isn't always easy.

Feet get tired, arms get tired,
hearts and hopes get tired.

Sometimes problems seem too big or complex.

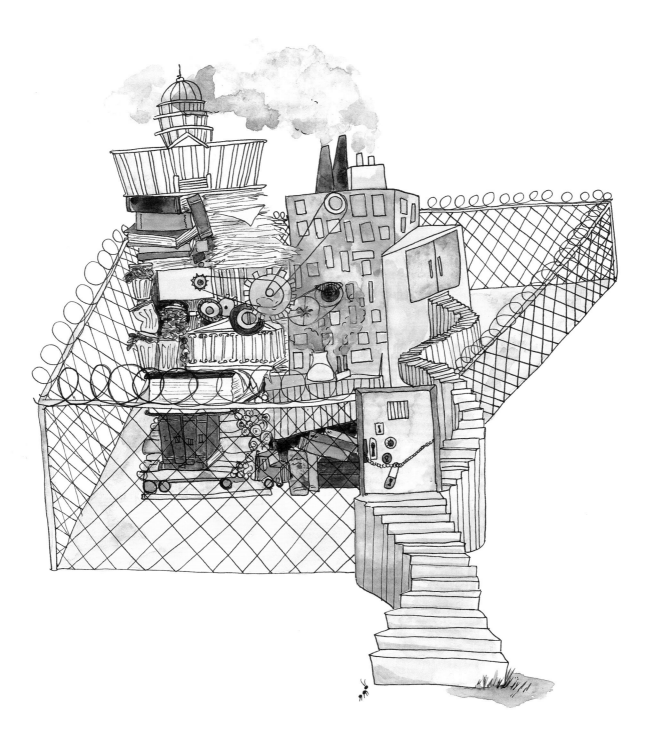

But we do not march alone.
Ants are stronger together.

Bands are louder together.

People are more powerful together.

Sometimes from feelings
of fear or anger or injustice
comes the hope for change.

Sometimes great change starts small,
with a brave question.

Maybe your question.
A question that calls
people together.

And together we find
the courage to march.

MOVEMENTS, MARCHES & KEY FIGURES IN THE ART:

Newsies strike, 1899: Hundreds of working kids went on strike to fight the unfair practices of their employers, New York's biggest newspapers. They won, and their protests inspired other labor strikes throughout the country (p. 19).

Garment workers' strike, 1909: During the industrial revolution, factories were notoriously dangerous. At the turn of the twentieth century, thousands of factory workers, mostly Jewish and immigrant women, marched for safer workplaces (p. 15).

NAACP's silent protest parade, 1917: Nearly 10,000 people gathered in New York City to protest the injustice against African Americans under Jim Crow laws in both the North and the South (p. 8).

Women's suffrage movement, 1776–1920: Since the founding of the United States women had been fighting for the right to vote. After many acts of resistance and marches, women finally won the right to vote in 1920 (p. 14).

Ida B. Wells (1862–1931): A writer and activist, Wells bravely documented the atrocities and violence committed against people of color in the South. Her work brought attention to the harsh realities of the Jim Crow era (p. 16).

Civil rights movement, 1950s–1960s: Through hundreds of marches, boycotts, and demonstrations, people all over country fought to end systemic racial injustice against people of color (p. 15).

Greensboro sit-ins, 1960 : Black students sat at the Woolworth's lunch counter to protest restaurants that would not serve people of color. These sit-in movements spread throughout the South (p. 19).

Selma to Montgomery march, 1965: Thousands of demonstrators marched from Selma to Montgomery, Alabama, to protest unjust laws that made it hard or impossible for people of color to vote. This march and the violence it confronted helped change voting rights laws across the United States (p. 20).

Delano grape boycott, 1960s: In 1965 Filipino and Mexican farmworkers united to fight for safe and fair working conditions (p. 18).

***Loving v. Virginia*, 1967:** Mildred Jeter, a woman of color, and Richard Loving, a white man, married in Washington, DC, in 1958, when interracial marriage was illegal in their home state of Virginia. When they moved back, they were arrested. They fought back, and eventually the Supreme Court ruled unanimously in 1967 that bans on interracial marriage are unconstitutional (p. 13).

***Tinker v. Des Moines Independent Community School District*, 1969:** Students in Des Moines, Iowa, were suspended for wearing black armbands to protest the Vietnam War. Eventually the Supreme Court ruled students and teachers kept their right to free speech even in school (p. 14).

Hudson River sloop *Clearwater*, 1960s–present: By the mid-twentieth century the Hudson River was terribly polluted. In 1966 musician and activist Pete Seeger and his friends began to sail up and down the Hudson River, singing about the beauty of nature and our need to protect it (p. 17).

Pride parade, 1970–present: Pride parades happen annually around the world to celebrate the LGBTQIA+ community and demonstrate for equal rights and acceptance (p. 14).

International Hotel, San Francisco, 1977: The International Hotel served as low-income housing for mostly elderly Filipino and Chinese immigrants, as well as a center of the Asian American community. When an eviction order was given to residents in 1977, 3,000 people linked arms to protect the hotel and the people who lived there (p. 24).

ACT UP, 1980s–present: This organization was founded to advocate for the health justice of people with HIV and AIDS, which disproportionately affected the gay community (p. 15).

Disability rights activism: Activists, beginning with Dorothea Dix, have been organizing for disability rights since the 1800s. Their work has led to huge changes in accessibility and care for people with mental and physical disabilities, including the Americans with Disabilities Act in 1990 (p. 14).

Occupy Wall Street movement, 2011: This multicity movement started in Zuccotti Park, New York City. It aimed to draw attention to, protest, and change economic inequality (p. 15).

March for Our Lives, 2018–present: This student-led march began in 2018, calling for an end to gun violence (p. 15).

Black Lives Matter movement, 2013–present: Black Lives Matter works to end police brutality and strives for the liberation of all Black lives (p. 14).

Kneeling protests, 2016–present: Some professional athletes kneel during the national anthem to protest systemic racism and police brutality (p. 19).

Dakota Access Pipeline protests, or #NoDAPL, 2016: People gathered on the Standing Rock Indian Reservation to protect the water that flows on the land where the Hunkpapa Lakota, Sihasapa Lakota, and Yanktoni Dakota people live (p. 12).

Immigration rights protests, 2016–present: Following the 2016 election, people around the country have gathered to fight policies of exclusion and make sure immigrants and their families are welcome and safe (pp. 15, 27).

Women's March, 2017: People around the country and the world marched for intersectional support of women's rights, LGBTQIA+ rights, immigration reform, health care and reproductive rights, and labor equality. (p. 15).

People's Climate March, 2017: People gathered all over the United States to protest the government's policies that harm the environment (p. 14).

Global Climate Strike, 2018–present: The Global Climate Strike began in 2018 as a student-driven protest and walkout demanding political action against the climate crisis (p. 15).

You can find out more about all of these organizations through their websites and learn more about the history of these movements through newspapers, museums, and archives and by talking to people who march in your community.